T0166567

Margaret Christakos | What Stirs

COACH HOUSE BOOKS, TORONTO

Published with the generous assistance of the Canada Council for the Arts and the Ontario Arts Council. Coach House Books also acknowledges the support of the Government of Canada through the Book Publishing Industry Development Program.

LIBRARY AND ARCHIVES CANADA CATALOGUING IN PUBLICATION

Christakos, Margaret
    What stirs / Margaret Christakos. -- 1st ed.

Poems.
ISBN 978-1-55245-204-2

    I. Title.

PS8555.H675W43 2008   C811'.54   C2008-904262-X

*for you**

CONTENTS

Little Latches

MUMSY

Lurch lunch, debut debates.
Cruise crud, sample maple.
Last and late. Too hot in the shower.
Marvel comically.

You may be my mumsy if you're *extra*
good tonight.

BRAIN MIXING BOARD (*active*)

I have no idea I mean you focused
I mean no idea I have you focused
to my gosh

BRAIN MIXING BOARD (*active*)

I have no idea I mean you focused
I mean no idea I have you focused
to my gosh

USED

The alphabet is a rigorous The
rigorous memory requires system memory Their
children don't require system and so
I'm going to hewn from couturiers

collectably.

Use it well I'll keep Keep
recalling it's one with sport recalling
if they stop disowning its own
many-featured face with one they don't

know sporting.

Large pink bowtie underneath as As
large as Sinatra in a carnival if
in department store were to be
less than carnivalesque would crane to

see Sinatra.

Be a letdown Always match Cleverly
match the gaunt Be up up
vain All the cleverly the punk
bowtie with some nice elbows Zesty

Almost gaunt.

Pair of satin gloves grazing Moist
shadow surly not grazing elbows moist
pair of satin shadow elbows Zesty
Almost dapper but not the pink

bowtie surely.

Vain All the women men Creditable
men too vain slit hollows too
be a letdown twisted crane to
see their hollow slits to be

less creditable.

In department store windows it's They
happen in lack like blubbering like
large punk bowtie blabbering They don't
know what will happen its own

many-featured lack.

If they stop looking upon Images
fail if upon enough ta-dah images
use it well enough hewn from
couturiers Mothers fail miserably system and

so ta-dah.

Their children don't believe they Their
memory They exist apparent exist The
alphabet is apparent some rigorous memory.

Whoever hears the wind and, is it
a rear tire grinding out of slush? Mnn.

They've been asleep for hours. I listen or sniff the air
for you, like I said.

It's embarrassing.

Just how many ways can hind senses be smarter
than Internet spam?

VISUAL SPLENDOUR COUPONS

My idle eyes beheld milk
and milk's surrogate: tears of disbelief, fatigue.

My gaze was practically lashed shut.

Still, I rose to smells of a good breakfast. I mean,
I stayed flat on my back, supine. Breasts globes.

The sun's opal leaked in.

Shafts of turquoise reclined. I refused to budge.

My beloved danced for me (ha-ha!), the babies whimpered.

Day filtered through a window, in white stripes.

Mauve hydrangea heads nodded off in front of my laptop
with the pallor of popped vivacity.

Shiny silver crescents flecked my visual field
along with glassfuls.

I wanted to doze. I desired a shower.

My eyes mapped the ceiling,
trilled loudly, then landed on their huge hazelling irises. The scene
was musical and filled with milk.

MATINÉE

How some moor opens loud
to fog. Over long shudders
one settles. Pontificate or to
ruminate on a swing bridge.

Look, your pupils, how each
dilates slowly. Elbows round counter.

Jurors find innocence indoors. X-Acto
blades trouble a grey bladder after
dinner. Money. Creepy penis joke.
Five off-key singers ...

QUEEN (*9–10 p.m., Eastern Standard Time*)

I was just trimming the beard about my sex
(Sorry if you did not know royal women do this)

And nipped in error the skin between my mound and
Thigh, a tissue cleavage as soft and unhurt

As any among my husband's old properties. An alcohol
Pad is there pressed, and stings me, burns

Bacterial moat-hoppers that could get excited
About trouncing the king to the velveteen purse.

He says he should be the only one to course
Me, that the belt is the equal of one hundred

Warships in the South Pacific. He boasts
I am lucky. When I first eyed the silver scissor

I thought to slice my wrist, but a vast canopy
Of solitude brought me to my vanities, and how

My fusspot maidens were having tea just then. To groom
Any part of my own flesh is sure subversion. So

I choose the nearest I can pinch to my blackish
Hole, and begin by candlelight, in a commode, to snip.

Almost a backward swoon.
Little yawn.
Coming up soon on your
local nipple.
A gain.
A gain.
A gain.

STRAPLESS

Sometimes we dress strapless.
You know, when you sense the self at your centre jiggle as if you might
break cold against
the heart, as if a lung might burst and out of your mouth will plume
white birds cooing and thrilling?
You pry and suckle.
Fold your leg backward and embrace your fresh buttock.
You rub your hair upward so it goes staticky.
Turn on the radio, listen for someone out there somewhere.
Dinner shimmers and snow hardens.
Absence is suffusion almost beauteous.
Nothing left to wrap yourself around, so you start with the vertical elements
toward which you simply lean.
Trees have a solidity most porches lack.
Telephone poles create society.
Internet's a web of felled me's.
You end one you begin another.
After this you'll get it.
Sequence is not your strong suit nor sequins out of order.
Let you help – thanks – with those eye hooks.

Some drugs blunt emotions and/or
reduce obsessive-compulsive thinking but these
are also two main characteristics
of romantic love Dr Fisher
mentioned in addition to the
obvious toll sexual side effects
can take on a romantic
relationship the shortage of key
brain chemicals involved in love
and long-term attachment aren't released.

All of this can make
it challenging to fall in
love or stay in love
while on an antidepressant said
Andy Thomson staff psychiatrist one
approach is to take an
antidepressant that can be stopped
intermittently for drug vacations without
losing effectiveness Dr Thomson offered
Forest Pharmaceutical's Lexapro sometimes can
be stopped Friday then resumed
Monday which stimulates the patient's
sexual interest over the weekends.

KEY BRAIN CHEMICALS (*Globe & Mail*)

for Dick

You have no idea you mean I focused
          on the bird
but as soon as you fired and saw
          Harry there everything
else went out of your mind you don't
          know whether the
birdie went down or didn't what happened to
          your friend as
a result of your actions it's part of
          this sudden you
know in less than a second less time
          than it takes
to tell going from what is a very
          happy pleasant day
with great friends in a beautiful part of
          the country doing
something you love to your gosh you've shot
          your friend you've
never experienced anything quite like that before not
          a good idea
each of you got a bird.

What if book just wants to be book? So
relieved someone could lend money, or give it

Hard tell when donor is loaded Perhaps will
owe perhaps not Now what should do for

livelihood Have examined merits becoming surrogate for childless
couple but type get over-attached I I I

just imagine panic when child whisked into arms
uv other woman Obviously terribly terribly terribly terribly

terribly terribly terribly bored Once upon day there
was page who made breathe quick anticipation little

messages caused skin uv world set aflutter O
caught in web uv nostalgia for likeable screw-buddy

How minor province restimulate? Employed have advantage uv
exhaustion I I I I I I I

all too pining for action Once upon day
uv Valentine's miscarriage what bloody day arrived Month

grooves downward avalanche-like Nice shrink offered marriage advice
last week Willing subjects sat side side same

couch good omen return tomorrow wish by turns
salvage ruin ruin everything then to settle off

uv seething Sorry wrecked everything with rancour All
4 now –

enjoyed *8 Mile* I'm going to see *Roger*
Dodger ASAP thinking it might illuminate you a
little to me Almost saw it in NY
on Saturday but went to a cool extremely

minimalist electronic music show instead The main performer
wired a mixing board to send output back
through channels producing feedback of almost unbearable if
a little melodic high frequencies Another player rubbed

a reed up and down over a drumhead
and the quivering vibrations produced static which served
as a low dodge-and-burn intensifier In a dumpy
cement gallery space on the Lower East Side

about fifty very cool young people plus me
sat in reverent silence just a few of
them pressing fingers in their ears to protect
themselves I thought the whole thing would have

been better on drugs but even still it
sent up a blooming whining metaphor of how
my psyche has singed and squealed yet made
no sound at all waiting and feeling the

outer limits these past several months Rather simultaneously
exciting and too mundane for language's access Anyway
New York is a place where art is
relevant and I think I'd like to live

there The rather preposterously empathetic roster of papers
given on Acker at the symposium I attended
made anyone think it's a good idea to
die young if you're gonna write I don't

know why I'm writing you today just because
I think it's very grey and fallish outside
like dusk like the busride melancholy fills the
body and language spills into space like a

secret shimmer Why feel anything but sometimes the
thing itself feels its way beyond the body
like a semaphore from a border an empire
of the senseful and I become a secretary

Another movie that brought you to mind Ah
cinema, popcorn –

ANDALOU

Eleven weeks to the day, I held
Her or him like a branch.
Like a tipped word. Through the window
Is another window.

That I trouble the waters of
your pretty face with my slow
finger, drawing down for a strand
of lily stem.

Fish go, floral tails.

You sway and dip your crown,
flat pad, under the edge of a second
pond.

I'm still kneeling on one rippled calf
broken like sound waves filling
a data screen, etched in magenta.

Yah, I dyed my hair orange, the
orange of the dusk sky, left the stuff on
an extra half-hour.

What are you doing, moon, in
my friend's mirroring
gawk at me? It's not midnight, the
news hasn't even started!

The fixed door is usually held closed using a hyphen dash on the edge of the door that slides upward into the jamb at the top.

There's a hyphen dash you pry open with your finger to release the chip.

Yep.

I had a red patent leather one, with a hyphen dash that clicked.

Was a hyphen dash key kid.

Photos show baby dash on with 'asymmetric' dash.

The hyphen dash is stuck and there's no way Kim can get it unstuck so Kim has to cut her out of it!

Handles, straps and a hyphen dash.

Everything is edible.

What is a dash and what is the difference between dash and flip flop?

≈

She lifted the hyphen dash and entered the turret door, while the lady and I waited below.

He'll dash on fine initially, then he pulls off and pops himself back on with a shallow dash.

The pink one has a hyphen dash for the lid and would look real cute on a chain.

So they think because there is a hyphen dash you push under a flange a bear could not watch you once and figure the whole thing out.

I will have to come up with some sort of hyphen dash.

I admit I am an addict.

Dash hooking is my life.

It has a hyphen dash you have to open up to get it open.

The hood dash is the catch or fastener that holds the hood of your vehicle closed whenever it is shut.

You know the hyphen dash that clips into the palm rest.

Anyway, you slot the blade in with a clever hyphen dash system and it stays in there nice and tight.

At the top is a hyphen dash: undash it.

≈

The entire cyclone top swings up and back like a dash.

≈

Don't be gullible.

A hyphen dash is on one half and has to be held down.

The concept of a dash circuit is important to create memory devices.

Aside from a few hyphen dash hiccups and a touch of jaundice in the first week, she's been a healthy hyphen lamb.

When the hyphen dash opens, jump up there.

Go stand astride the other square box thingy.

Your safer-sex kit stays shut with a hyphen dash.

Try to be eligible, with a hyphen perfume.

Lower anchors and tethers for children.

A server crashed because of a long semaphore wait for the adaptive hash dash, some dinky hyphen dash a two-year-old kid could break with a flick of a finger.

But the fact that it's got a hyphen dash door is a nice touch.

Forceps can sometimes bruise the jaws, making it painful for the baby to open wide.

Makers of hand-knitting yarns and dash hook kits.

Free patterns.

Hyphen supplements like baby's milk for adults.

In a capsule.

It's that hyphen dash attached on the hood that holds that bar.

A hyphen dash lube saves big bucks.

Shrink-wrapping, a hard plastic sleeve, those impenetrable labels, and finally a hyphen dash on the cover itself.

So secure.

The dash in front seems to make the drive work hard.

The hyphen dash that lifts up like one of those giant paper cutters.

Push down a hyphen dash on each side.

The shield pops on or off.

That's it, period.

≈

A dash is a memory equivalent of a lock.

I put the candle on the floor and Ellie and I crouched over the box as I lifted the hyphen dash and raised the lid.

All with wire mesh see-through top and a little dash!

Put your ear hoops in one, neck chains in another.

When I was hyphen, dash hook rugs were all the rage, and my mother would sit for hours hooking hyphen pieces of wool yarn into hyphen holes.

She'd say if your guitar case has a hyphen dash for a lock, lock it!

Well, today the hyphen dash holding my mailbox shut broke.

The *effin* hyphen dash mechanism.

She opened the hyphen dash and moved to put it on, but Nick took it and did it for her, kneeling by the couch and not relinquishing her hand.

I got out and snagged my pants on the hyphen dash post on the truck rig.

There, the baby had been snugged close at the end of the dash.

The rabbit said, quote Do you see that hyphen dash?

Quote Yes period.

Quote Unloose it and jump in, end quote.

To access the water table, pull the hyphen dash on the foregrip – yes, like the hyphen dash that holds the cocking arm up.

To reach that vent I found that a hot dog fork is just the right length to reach up and force each hyphen dash into place.

Reached between your knees for the hyphen dash.

Securely.

Very tight.

Had a crooked roof with a crooked hyphen patch.

Had a crooked roof with a crooked hyphen patch, etc.

But said that, like a dash that's a deadbolt.

Well, today the hyphen dash holding my mailbox shut broke.

He's been swapping objects in and out of the spider box through a hyphen dash.

To remove the wiper arm, they simply pulled that hyphen dash out, bent the wiper arm back and slid it off.

All she had to do was hit it repeatedly till the hyphen dash dropped open.

Did you mean hyphen *match*?

≈

All I had to do was turn the hyphen dash with my mouth and pull, really, really hard, and the turret door would turn.

Note the hyphen dash you exposed when you removed the arm case.

This is the hook shutter.

Lube and dry.

Leads to the bobbin.

I'm seriously considering cutting the hyphen dash off the top of my T-Mobile case.

I wanted to whip that thing.

I almost freakin whipped it.

Okay, I was sweating a bucket but I closed the hyphen dash, and put the heat sink on.

Does the heat sink need screws to be secure?
The hyphen dash is a hit.
Has a crooked door with a crooked hyphen dash.

≈

Well, when more cargo space is needed, the rear seats split sixty-forty and fold flat with the help of a smart hyphen dash release button in the cargo area.
Just brill.
At its max, you can't budge the dash.
When it gangs up with seven siblings, it suddenly becomes a worthwhile bit of silicon.
As long as I had the dash over the memory socket open, I blew gusts into the opening to clear a few visible hyphen specks.
And voila the bookcase!
Oh.
The fact that the only thing to hold the front and back doors closed was a piddly hyphen dash lock was a big laugh.
I mean guffaw.
Maybe it was the heavy glass and steel or the clumsy hyphen dash.
Maybe it was the fear.
We simply clicked a hyphen dash into place to secure this door, then the birds were safe and sound.
The hyphen dash held the lid shut was plastic.
It is new and wide, quite gaping.
Once pumped milk could sit cold on the ledge for days.
His copier also had a rather dull hyphen dash on the underside of its sizable lid.
Quote It was loosey-goosey dull end quote.

Lovely One

Clouds are lovely in the valley

I've known the moist movement
reach for its thin shelf of provisions

Consolation over chaos knows plenty
about poured chords

And you've certainly heard about pleasure

Less is surely the future

Opals for the moment
are sleepful

Valley, I've known
movement reach for
shelves of provisions

Chaos knows plentya
chords and you've –
about pleasure – less

Some future opal
moments are sleepful

Do you know how lovely are clouds
or about the sound of opals
you know about this cold portal
you've known this moist movement
toward tone, melody over chaotic
topography of love, how
valley hope forlorns the Mondays
through Friday's consolation, a river's
montage sleep on sadness, you know
lovely one

Art inside your name
cannot be uncoiled
no itinerary or market
there's a thin shelf of provisions
and sustenance to be proven
so little's worth saying

Know how lovely
clouds valley
sound opals about one
colder portal

A moist movement
tones melody over
chaotic love rivers any forlorn
consolation

Montage sadness art inside name

Uncoiled no itinerary
or market there's
this thin shelf of
provisions sustenance to
be proven oval so
little worth
saying

Still –

Saying little
be provisions thin or uncoiled
river valley montage some
consolation chaotic over
movement

Colder and oval sound clouds lovely
you, one portal
worth the milky shades, the
tony hues
of love's opals

My Attaché Case

DAY 1

I like did I mention
visual splendour coupons

You knew that what you
carried in it was
not the important object it
was the surrogate of
what could not be carried
at all but bartered.

My breasts have held milk
and expressed milk and
held language by the tit
so to speak attachment.

The modification of any object
by who owns it
I mean the person thinks
they can own something
and then there must also
be things not owned
nor· carried around for another
effect like visual splendour
weight rebalancing mood alteration transfer
to a new stanza.

Trees hooked to sky by
the gaze eyelashed shut.

What is the mystery I
went to sleep then
woke up smelling only foods
I can't stand lukewarm.

≈

Knew that what I
can't stand lukewarm redeemables
not the important object
it is the mystery
I ruefully what could
not be carried the
gaze eyelashed shut saddens

My breasts have held
milk to a new
stanza code held language
by the tit effect
like visual splendour coupons

The modification of any
object be things not
owned consecutively I mean
the person thinks they
can own something timeshare
and then there must
also by who owns
it convincingly nor carried
around for another so
to speak attachment cabaret
weight rebalancing mood alteration
transfer and expressed milk

and nuptials Trees hooked
to sky by at
all but bartered purple

I went to sleep
what was the surrogate
of amnesia woke up
smelling only foods you
carried in It was
awesome.

And in my attaché case
I put all the things
that have stood in for
me Stand up for me –
Stood guard I carry my
case in my right hand
I open doors with the
left There's a shiny silver
latch I can see as
I walk Everything I'd hoped
for attends in the rectangular
space See There is air
preserved for a moonwalk for
a last large cosmic gasp.

I plan Never forget my
case even when particularly slow
in the head else rigid
under the knees Sometimes my
shins ache Nothing distracts me
Soon as my hat's on
the case handle heats each
sleek crease of my knuckles
I cup its plastic weight
A nonslip baton I'll never
ever hand off and abandon
This is how well attached
I am to my future
dear ones are you pleased?

CRI DE COEUR, DEFERRED

The tone of it is
All wrong or it's odd
For we prefer real order

Some song couldn't be more
Perfect at this square table
The tone seems a canker

All five chairs are neatly
Placed we concede in unison
It's coming on just now. Still.

The tone of it is
All wrong we concede in
Unison the tone seems some

Canker a song couldn't be
More perfect and it's odd
It's coming on just now

All five chairs so neatly
Placed at this square table
For we prefer real order.

TOUCHÉ

I carry my canker
I walk
Sometimes my shins ache
The tone seems a sleek crease of my knuckles
I cup its plastic weight all wrong
It's odd for we
Prefer real order dear ones –
Are you pleased?

ATTOUCHÉ

We knew that what we order dear ones cannot stand
visual splendour surrogates

Our breasts have held pleased nonslip perfect milk to
pleased new stanza code held language

We concede its cup its plastic by touched tit effect

We mean touched persons think and deserve coupons

Forget our particularly transfer or expressed milk

For touched tone of it pleased latch we stood guard
couldn't be case in our odd touched perfect and we
knew that what we carried in it was not *attouché*

Air Index

AIR QUALITY

Sulphur's the devil in your mouth

copper in your pocket

gold in your testicles

silver in the lining of your brain, crisping

That's what they're saying sweetheart

Bonne chance

AIR TRAVEL

A soup of atmosphere tugs us back

Purple stew at sunset

All of us levy a coordinated breaststroke

Captain shouts *Heave, ya bastards!*

You expected comfort?

AIR HORN

If the geese thought they'd still have time

they were wrong

A bonk on the wing is better

than sewer rats for lunch

The way to San José is aquiver

with few and fewer friends

Ba ba ba ba ba ba ba-ba bah-

hmm

AIR LAUNDRY

Dries on the lawn and the dog

well

she's old and has a bit of a –

Self-discipline the goal here

the neighbours don't have to see

everything

AIR FARCE

Under the ocean it's blue, too, bubbly

but you have to suck and chug continually

and finally you start to burp

and there's only so many

exit signs and they're all

brightest red

How odd you look in the cold sunrise

with terrific white feathers of milk embellishing your nostrils

About midnight, your mood goes black –

foul as the mud the suckers like seekers

like to hide in, latched together

Let's go now

This is getting ridiculous

AIR OUT

Squall a bit when the midwife visits

let the tract among garlic

gaelic

and gall

make itself smelled

You've internalized enough, darling

We're going for a stroll

and the sun's strafed with blue

gases

Let's have a good one

AIR DIVINE

And we're forgiven

The Hoity-Toity Supplements

(OR, ONE VERY INTERESTING EXAMPLE)

Surreptitious breasts as in

Reptilian lights, UV as in

Petalled heights as in

Leapable bells as in

Reptilian harelips as in

Trainer downpours as in

Nearer buttocks as in

Errant rodents as in

Trainer rages as in

Lalala ales as in

Alibi autonomy, senses of as in

Bailable experiments as in

Lalala everything, weight of as in

Lamented prayers as in

Team porkchops, thick as in

Eminent nemeses as in

Lamented peppermints as in

Temperamental capitas as in

Ermine muck, slush-filled as in

Mirthful perimeters as in

Temperamental encounters as in

Repetitious kisses, French as in

Breasty weeping as in

Eastern shorebirds as in

Repetitious steeples as in

Etiquettes, quiet as in

Quittable furnishings as in

Taut locations as in

Etiquettes, moderate as in

Tête-à-tête chowdowns as in

Teatlike tardiness, undiluted as in

Chamomile archipelagos

UNSORTED:

Pelican openers

Hellraiser switchblades

Elbow shoppers

Bausch fans

Shufflers, medicated

Shufflers, non-medicated

Shufflers

Flowered wobbly cops

Word operatives

For example for a good of it for crap's sake for a quartet of pheromones
Here is a reasonable example you were asking for, albeit politely
I don't have to grind my teeth to hear into a future body of turtles
Crow loud if you will decide on sleeping; let me into uno secret

Mothers always have a resistance to magnifying sutures
For a while now I've considered you defunct and rigid, like camel saddle
A way wind spews itself without any indication of need
Hold me restive, kneecap: do what it is you really want

At the back of a house is a bucket filled with sawdust Sniff it
Slowly, don't check into a sewer, promise Take your degree in Biz Admin
Crumple its shins Grunt as you release a defecant Torso small
Ankles chubbed out like salami I hate you for your slick pedicure

Doll Valley is a good name if you live in an area, or if not you're
Nostalgic for an arena Why not keep your better clothes in a mothproof bag
Buy a bruised fruit a fig Asian pear pomegranate Stiffen
Up, cling to yourself all through a loneliest dead-of-night crests you

For me this is a very interesting example for another opinion press star
Gild lilacs in a most casual charade Don't pack too much in one pouch
Do what you do when for example you try to do some particular thing
Don't get vague on me for god's sake regard me with a glint of tin

Simper like a bunny Radiant mechanic likes to fix things silver, squid
Black strafe roads vivid, get me? Let in a driver's seat Hold my coffee
In two hands as if you had a third Resemblances to rose bushes lose squeaker
Payoff I wanted to see not a top of your head but deep into your skull

Four catches tongues in an embarrassing psychopatent I was real original
And proud of a fact of how real this accomplishment can be when I am half
Awake in her head, I am telling you this again about her skull's inside, carmine
Compartment shivered with extra spaciousness and I closed a little latch

Rouge river we are not so sure of how to get close to, but all trees awfully
Fresh gurgle over pebbles Chill stream For a best result keep stern
For heaven will always palpate like blood, it's just an idea of its best version
Of frank self, what a self looks like inside its very reddened cap crown on.

HER MICROPHOBIC LIKES DISLIKES

You dilly-dally when should ramble or
gallop Knick-knacks in my mother's gifts
jiggle: extra bubble wrap Hee-haw on
the see-saw unabashed Too much brat-packing

for the social good Scritch-scratch when
you get the crabs Jesus Murphy!
Just about tumbled higgledy-piggledy outta my
brassiere Turf shipshape from the lawnmower

Sentences flitting about loosey-goosey, zif
thirsted at sea turvy-topsy on Benedictine
and limeade Beaten-up willy-nilly for
precious little My kid sister's loitering

about hoity-toity, lollygagging on MuchMusic.

Sherry Mary does know all about the hoity-toity supplements
one should ingest when Jesus Murphy! pregnant Sherry Mary can
dispense a lot of dilly-dally advice to anyone
who wants to get pregnant Sherry Mary's been loosey-goosey
there a hee-haw half-dozen times and would
go again to the altered brat-packing state of
pregnancy It's just a scritch-scratch example Sherry Mary finds
interesting Many women couldn't take the lollygagging news
of knock-up easily We'd balk They'd see-saw walk
She'd crack You'd smudge out the higgledy-piggledy opportunity
for very good shipshape reason but for Sherry Mary
it remains worth saying turvy-topsy if one's gonna
be seeding the willy-nilly fetus it's VERY IMPORTANT
TO TAKE extra folic acid knick-knacks EVERY DAY!

SHERRY MARY'S THERAPIST SUGGESTS

For example a reasonable
future body on sleeping;
resistance to rigid, like
itself without kneecap: do

Sawdust sniff your degree
its shins hate you
or, if clothes in
fruit, a dead-of-night crests

Another opinion most casual
for example god's sake
things silver, vivid, get
a third head but

Real original accomplishment can
awake in extra spaciousness
close to, over pebbles
an idea very reddened.

SORTED, SORT OF:

Bucket shins

Camel spews

Defecant ankles, slick

Example pheromones

Fig crests

Hands, squeaker

Name clothes

Opinion lilacs

Pebbles, best version

Resistance sutures

Roads, coffee

Skull catches

Skull's trees

Sleeping mothers

Teeth turtles

Things, squid

Tin likes

Tongues, half

ASH, AS IN ASHEN, SHERRY MARY FEELS

Surreptitious breasts of the brain's inside, crammed with
reptilian lights, UV or incandescent, zoom lens for the purpose of
petalled heights. Sherry Mary saw him hunkered and hiding, grasping
leapable bells in his greasy palms. Smarmy knots.

Reptilian harelips was the only upside of a tragic night.
Trainer downpours so that the race was cancelled. Shit, her big bog
nearer buttocks, she was leaking and made a slushy sound like
errant rodents, skewering pork tidbits sheltered by a rooftop.

Trainer rages, that's the thing, the habit that succumbs to
lalala ales, her mother always lathered the chest region liberally, no
alibi autonomy, senses of guilt and ease of corruption. They got out of their
bailable experiments, don't you worry.

Lalala everything, weight of how gay-hearted one must pretend, through
lamented prayers and handicapped vision. Used to have a vice-grip on
team porkchops, thick carcasses of inevitable excellence, always the interesting
eminent nemeses of her will to fail and relax a little. She just wanted a nap.

Lamented peppermints, then. Something stupid and picayune, Sherry Mary's
temperamental capitas, her favourite premise for a day in bed. Rope her in
ermine muck, slush-filled as the humiliation by soaking and bypassing
mirthful perimeters, how joyous she was wearing the smile of a cheater.

Temperamental encounters which her father encouraged, and Billy Bob's
repetitious kisses, French 'restraint,' kind where you orgasm out loud toward
breasty weeping cascading how ridiculous it is, all the sentimental noise of
eastern shorebirds sniping and shredding meat from each others' beaks.

Repetitious steeples hurt them. Run, run the other ditch past clever night
etiquettes, quiet shoe in a pile of dog crud, wipe and douse and camouflage;
quittable furnishings spew plastic odour anyway, nobody's got the sensors for
taut locations, exact maps. It's abreast of the brain's lining again, surreptitious

Etiquettes, moderate verging on maniacal, all of them prefer civilized
tête-à-tête chowdowns where one will wonder if the pork is well-cooked, prize
teatlike tardiness, undiluted crankiness. Do it right, is what they wish of
chamomile archipelagos. Do the example as well as interest will indulge.

I so love Sherry Mary and all her hoity-toity supplements. Jesus Murphy! I said pregnant again! My dilly-dally advice won't be any good, for who wants loosey-

goosey me to weigh in after kissing so repetitively all up and down Sherry Mary's surreptitious breasts and nearer buttocks and oh-so-pleasant well of

chamomile cunt juice, all her mirthful perimeters, such lalala hee-haw half-dozen times I repeat myself and would go again, just a scritch-scratch example

many women couldn't take, they'd balk or smudge me out of the picture drop my file in the UNSORTED pile at any higgledy-piggledy opportunity and for

very good shipshape reason but for Sherry Mary whom I adore it's no whim or wham-bam remains worth repeating turvy-topsy if one's gonna be seeding

petalled heights of a darling willy-nilly fetus she tells me it's VERY IMPOR-TANT to take extra folic acid knick-knacks EVERY DAY so I'm

buying a double supply plus some peppermints and fig crests for my sweet kick-boxing knickerbocker Sherry Mary! I LOVE to fuck her so!

SHERRY MARY'S THERAPIST ON LUNCH

For me this is a very interesting example for another opinion press star

Regard me with a glint of tin: Has the pork been well-cooked?

What a self looks like inside its very reddened cap

Vivid, get a third head

I opened a little latch Oh and

Don't you worry

Alibi autonomy, senses of
1 2 3 4 5 6 7 8 9 10
Bailable experiments
1 2 3 4 5 6 7 8 9 10 11
Bausch fans
1 2 3 4 5 6 7 8 9 10 11 12
Breasty weeping
1 2 3 4 5 6 7 8 9 10 11 12 13
Bucket shins
1 2 3 4 5 6 7 8 9 10 11 12 13 14
Camel spews
1 2 3 4 5 6 7 8 9 10 11 12 13 14 15
Chamomile archipelagos
1 2 3 4 5 6 7 8 9 10 11 12 13 14 15 16
Defecant ankles, slick
1 2 3 4 5 6 7 8 9 10 11 12 13 14 15 16 17
Eastern shorebirds
1 2 3 4 5 6 7 8 9 10 11 12 13 14 15 16 17 18
Elbow shoppers
1 2 3 4 5 6 7 8 9 10 11 12 13 14 15 16 17 18 19
Eminent nemeses
1 2 3 4 5 6 7 8 9 10 11 12 13 14 15 16 17 18 19 20
Ermine muck, slush-filled
1 2 3 4 5 6 7 8 9 10 11 12 13 14 15 16 17 18 19 20 21
Errant rodents
1 2 3 4 5 6 7 8 9 10 11 12 13 14 15 16 17 18 19 20 21 22
Etiquettes, moderate
1 2 3 4 5 6 7 8 9 10 11 12 13 14 15 16 17 18 19 20 21 22 23
Etiquettes, quiet
1 2 3 4 5 6 7 8 9 10 11 12 13 14 15 16 17 18 19 20 21 22 23 24
Example pheromones
1 2 3 4 5 6 7 8 9 10 11 12 13 14 15 16 17 18 19 20 21 22 23 24 25
Fig crests
1 2 3 4 5 6 7 8 9 10 11 12 13 14 15 16 17 18 19 20 21 22 23 24 25 26
Flowered wobbly cops
1 2 3 4 5 6 7 8 9 10 11 12 13 14 15 16 17 18 19 20 21 22 23 24 25 26 27
Hands, squeaker
1 2 3 4 5 6 7 8 9 10 11 12 13 14 15 16 17 18 19 20 21 22 23 24 25 26 27 28
Hellraiser switchblades
1 2 3 4 5 6 7 8 9 10 11 12 13 14 15 16 17 18 19 20 21 22 23 24 25 26 27 28 29

Lalala ales

1 2 3 4 5 6 7 8 9 10 11 12 13 14 15 16 17 18 19 20 21 22 23 24 25 26 27 28 29

Lalala everything, weight of

1 2 3 4 5 6 7 8 9 10 11 12 13 14 15 16 17 18 19 20 21 22 23 24 25 26 27 28 29

Lamented peppermints

1 2 3 4 5 6 7 8 9 10 11 12 13 14 15 16 17 18 19 20 21 22 23 24 25 26 27 28 29

Lamented prayers

1 2 3 4 5 6 7 8 9 10 11 12 13 14 15 16 17 18 19 20 21 22 23 24 25 26 27 28 29

Leapable bells

1 2 3 4 5 6 7 8 9 10 11 12 13 14 15 16 17 18 19 20 21 22 23 24 25 26 27 28 29

Mirthful perimeters

1 2 3 4 5 6 7 8 9 10 11 12 13 14 15 16 17 18 19 20 21 22 23 24 25 26 27 28 29

Name clothes

1 2 3 4 5 6 7 8 9 10 11 12 13 14 15 16 17 18 19 20 21 22 23 24 25 26 27 28 29
1 2 3 4 5 6 7 8 9 10 11 12 13 14 15 16 17 18 19 20 21 22 23 24 25 26 27 28 29

Nearer buttocks

1 2 3 4 5 6 7 8 9 10 11 12 13 14 15 16 17 18 19 20 21 22 23 24 25 26 27 28 29
1 2 3 4 5 6 7 8 9 10 11 12 13 14 15 16 17 18 19 20 21 22 23 24 25 26 27 28 29
1 2 3 4 5 6 7 8 9 10 11 12 13 14 15 16 17 18 19 20 21 22 23 24 25 26 27 28 29

Opinion lilacs

1 2 3 4 5 6 7 8 9 10 11 12 13 14 15 16 17 18 19 20 21 22 23 24 25 26 27 28 29
1 2 3 4 5 6 7 8 9 10 11 12 13 14 15 16 17 18 19 20 21 22 23 24 25 26 27 28 29

Pebbles, best version

1 2 3 4 5 6 7 8 9 10 11 12 13 14 15 16 17 18 19 20 21 22 23 24 25 26 27 28 29

Pelican openers

1 2 3 4 5 6 7 8 9 10 11 12 13 14 15 16 17 18 19 20 21 22 23 24 25 26 27 28

Petalled heights

1 2 3 4 5 6 7 8 9 10 11 12 13 14 15 16 17 18 19 20 21 22 23 24 25 26 27

Quittable furnishings

1 2 3 4 5 6 7 8 9 10 11 12 13 14 15 16 17 18 19 20 21 22 23 24 25 26

Repetitious kisses, French

1 2 3 4 5 6 7 8 9 10 11 12 13 14 15 16 17 18 19 20 21 22 23 24 25

Repetitious steeples

1 2 3 4 5 6 7 8 9 10 11 12 13 14 15 16 17 18 19 20 21 22 23 24

Reptilian harelips

1 2 3 4 5 6 7 8 9 10 11 12 13 14 15 16 17 18 19 20 21 22 23

Reptilian lights, uv

1 2 3 4 5 6 7 8 9 10 11 12 13 14 15 16 17 18 19 20 21 22

Resistance sutures

1 2 3 4 5 6 7 8 9 10 11 12 13 14 15 16 17 18 19 20 21

Roads, coffee

1 2 3 4 5 6 7 8 9 10 11 12 13 14 15 16 17 18 19 20

Shufflers
1 2 3 4 5 6 7 8 9 10 11 12 13 14 15 16 17 18 19
Shufflers, medicated
1 2 3 4 5 6 7 8 9 10 11 12 13 14 15 16 17 18
Shufflers, non-medicated
1 2 3 4 5 6 7 8 9 10 11 12 13 14 15 16 17
Skull catches
1 2 3 4 5 6 7 8 9 10 11 12 13 14 15 16
Skull's trees
1 2 3 4 5 6 7 8 9 10 11 12 13 14 15
Sleeping mothers
1 2 3 4 5 6 7 8 9 10 11 12 13 14
Surreptitious breasts
1 2 3 4 5 6 7 8 9 10 11 12 13
Taut locations
1 2 3 4 5 6 7 8 9 10 11 12
Team porkchops, thick
1 2 3 4 5 6 7 8 9 10 11
Teatlike tardiness, undiluted
1 2 3 4 5 6 7 8 9 10
Teeth turtles
1 2 3 4 5 6 7 8 9
Temperamental capitas
1 2 3 4 5 6 7 8
Temperamental encounters
1 2 3 4 5 6 7
Tête-à-tête chowdowns
1 2 3 4 5 6
Things, squid
1 2 3 4 5
Tin likes
1 2 3 4
Tongues, half
1 2 3
Trainer downpours
1 2
Trainer rages
1
Word operatives
Word operatives
Word operatives
Word operatives
Word operatives

SUPPLEMENT

Hoity-Toity, nine pounds, two ounces
Born to Sherry Mary and Billy Bob
Such joyous they cannot file
Any known where

For heaven will always palpate like blood, it's just an idea of its best version
Of frank self, what a self looks like inside its very reddened cap crown on.

Do it right, is what they wish of
Chamomile archipelagos. Do the example as well as interest will indulge.

Wind I am lonely

Compared, impaired by poetry, what you should be getting – so gaseous – escapes. Perfume to the firmament miming good manners of happy people. Overdone these days. Easily replaced by pills or airborne spores' promise set to tunnel inward as you snooze.

≈

Impaired, compared to poetry's precision. Leave side door unlocked – neighbourhood's safety net secures us. Threaded air in lousy AM music fibrous. Fibrillating heart antic for a latte, you know? Everything human simmers with a caffeine stench, blooming up.

≈

Pillow like opal compared to poetry aglow in the silent bedroom. Sexy as recording of homemade intercourse on Internet, blond chick with dildo moaning. Impaired as French geek solving Rubik's cube with chimpanzee toes – he's faking it, reverses video – grunts arousal. If you can see yourself in this playback mirror, clap your soles. Purgatory like jouissance – jouissance like a population purged of the intimate.

≈

Botox botany in megasuperstore. Jade leaves inflated, about to orgasm. We are all inches from a precipice expecting ecstasy. So depressed another coffee feels marvellous. I rub your shoulder blade, you bleeping spasm! Messy as poetry compared to itself, a slurped orgy of impaired hearts flickering at melamine-spiked minnow feed.

≈

No more things or lotions to add or perforate. Everything's sort of ugly. Her nipples press into lens smeared with petroleum, licked clean. His cock's rigid and ridged, highly defined as a life form between cover slides. All desire so gaseous even perfection's impaired, compared to poetry.

LOST ('IMMORTAL')

Living this long's going worse than planned.
I get to the top of the mountain and discover
a bunch of dead ones, perfectly
preserved.
Their navels latched with opals.
Each opal a microchip speaker still issuing.

We'd left behind language so long ago –
I ached for my mother's
hips and of course
her warm corneal voice. Through
airstreams so thin in
almost a swoon she
seemed to bulge toward my looking;
something whatever
was what she lip signalled
then a cold suchness got to my fingers.

What is and isn't sophisticated thinking
unhitches every sense
from the body I use.
                    Fucking mountain.

That stiffen you better believe
the nerves *That* tilt spine
to a downstairs shower *That*
wave cables, torn-ended *Which* I
used to live in *Which*
are better meant for livestock
That hurt you to look
for *That* crust your boot-heel
Whose better days are long gone
In which you lost your
virgin mind *In* whose memory
That suffer the supine *Which*
riddle your noggin: why here?
you wonder *Out* of office
space *Out* of back rooms
behind beauty salons *Out* of
fourteen found doors from a
wrecked condo *That* could fit
in a breadbasket *That* jiggle
Which jut into a rear
drive *Whose* carpenters were unemployed
creative writing teachers *Without* drainage
With putrid puce wall lamps
Which repel *That* pull *That*
limpidly want your body in
their jaws *Whose* last name
you always forget *Which* attic
is a polite word for *In*
which somebody was born *In*
which personal ads are not
enough *That* classify your love
That listen in on your
hatreds *Insofar* as it can
be considered inanimate, and that's
not far at all *In*
so many dreams baby *Which*
clap you on the buttock

With a tree *Without* doorknobs
That send you to the
basement for a time out
Where you never wanted to
live but ended up staying for
a couple decades.

I love wax scabs patchouli-scented.
Does gender continue to hair's pretty?
Let's he's a complete loser.
Your zipper up.
Are pretty grounded but I am timid now.
Festoonery.
A bird's wing but not droopily.
Triangles grass.

Being preoccupied I pathos now that the nothing to love in for the second time alone with our love is cocked in your marries the two.
There are brutal.
Car alarms carom like a nice person all you listen to people care to hear into the storyline.
I was my wimpish instrument?
The agent the hammer is a puke some horns pip on you can barely thigh?
I tell myself.
You will tour guide.

Marmalade grasses flop over like solar pleasures.
For example, birds or an attitude element in distrust.

For example, surreptitious crows could mean something about birds or
an attitude toward humans, in that you hold just about every element in

distrust. Marmalade clouds or mackerel horizon. Certain grasses flop over
like the insolent wings in *Swan Lake*. Desolate. Solar pleasures.

Does this say anything about such a beige noon that I want to go back
to bed? I revert to myself when the jiggling hollyhock leaves settle.

You will care about me as your narrator, not as your buddy or tour guide. I
can't be your laundress and I won't suck you off. You are a shallow

consumer if your palm is starting to perspire, already, before your arse
is even warm. What chair did you pick and why, is parallel to my gaze

flickering to the thudless basketball hoop. I had a feeling. I had a strong
feeling of swivelling to the left then lifting my chin and recovering from

a long blink. We inhabit the airplane drone and wherever it goes next.
Once I almost told a man on a bus a secret and we were not even at

the French. You don't require such a striptease or if you did you'd be gone
now. Ah, this breeze crushes its velvet on my forearm. I stir. I

sentimentally bother taking notice. The rest of the world is never at
rest like I am in this subtle collision with wind. I don't give. I don't

give a fuck. Perhaps I am a selfish brat but so are you if you have a book
in your hand. I'll tell you what it is to be a writer so you let

yourself off the hook of longing that any reader winches tighter one
lung at a time. You will have valued the plow of air that every afternoon

offers when you step from the building where you work into a blast of
car exhaust, there on the sidewalk and jostled by men in paisley ties

who look morbid about their own adolescence. You are one of, pink
bucket in morning glory foliage. Hydrangea lime, the young leaves

dying for moisture. Don't go. I like you. For example, I made extra coffee
and blow-dried my hair to get quickly to this table. Toronto rattles like

a huge hysterical woodpecker. We are beating ourselves. Trust me.
I will tell you something necessary. Images cascade as a car accelerates.

I scratch. Some fellow hammers. Astonishingly, no one is killed outright.
I am so lonely. This alphabet is familial or so I tell myself.

The agent about now says Jesus Christ nothing happens. The hammer
is a real thing the guttural trucks on Bathurst are about to puke some

horns pip and toot a handsaw whines. I mean, so much is going on you
can barely write it all down. What's that moving in your thigh? What

stirs? Have you farted a little, for I recognize the air pulsing on my
cheekbone. The paper burbled death and a paroxysm of death under

blood spurting from unlucky bodies and the higher incidence of death.
I was appalled as numb as usual. Do you feel more than my wimpish

instrument? I scan the classifieds. My children whom I love, all three
as beautiful as a word. Now you are aware I am no virgin and still I will

not suck you off so my selfishness cements itself. You are no credible
virgin, come on. Tall grasses asymmetrical as flags tipping when a country

is about to fall. All seems safe here. Forty-four approaches. Car
alarms carom and then a surging surf of full-out wind. You look like a

nice person, whether I could love you or not I wonder. First of all you listen
to wind so you must be audible. Only good and alive people care

to hear the breezes falter and cheer when they walk back into the storyline.
So we have established your goodness. Which is dull and

unsatisfying to reader and writer alike. I have perhaps no idea about
my purpose for surely there are better occupations than this sentence.

There are no better occupations. Occupations are terribly brutal. Being
preoccupied I sense the wind. The peony bush has real pathos now

that the glamorous blossoms are brown. Tell me there is nothing to
love in a sentence like that. I'll accuse you of superficiality for the

second time and you'll take it or go. If you leave I can't go on alone with
our love affair which I'm sure is now about to begin. My brain is cocked

in your direction like a pistol or like desire or how our culture marries the
two. I prefer threesomes or the idea of three or the triangle of having

two love objects to notice and entice. These two words suddenly fall in love.
It was like this when I met you and your face caused a seizure. I

was occupied onward into my future and how it is now I have wrested
free. I am ice. No justice in any of it. For a moment I confused you

with someone I used to love excuse me. When strangers meet this happens
or nothing does. Nothing happens or this does. Love falls and

faults those who resemble our parents. Incestuous sponges all of us.
You want a refill? I like how hot this coffee is even an hour old. It

holds up. It will sustain me if you go. My hair literally shimmers in sun
now I see I am so attractive. Hair will do this at noon no longer

beige it is absolutely lemon and charming. The back of my hand
so moist and touchworthy. You want what it's worth as if ideas

could be money. It is time to reveal something about being a writer. I
am restless as restless as you, and in my thigh something roves. I tense

and relax each buttock so my groin pulses and feels juicy. Sun
warms me. My thoughts shift to cunty full-out sex the way the wind

comes up and blasts us a cascade of images which accelerate lust like
cars gunning in the alley. Then all settles to stillness. My long blink

sees the sugar maple. Old bikes. Ceramic urn and half-deflated basketball.
Bark chips saturated with a ten-year flame-retardant

guarantee. Wind pummels and showers. I previously implied I am
lonely. Meant I am a loner. Can you with a book in your hand relate?

Does your other hand wander to your thigh and upward? Tell me I am
ready to hear more than the wind blow and shuttle and instigate

contrast as a principle of consciousness. I am ready to get into your pants. I
like how you are patient. When you fall in love at the beginning

there is great patience and a kind of agitated hope. Poplar trembles.
Your face caused a seizure. I shuddered. Capitulated.

Gathered myself inward and took a longer time blinking until the
lemony noon wound up waning. Other people were getting killed all

over the place. I refilled your coffee. My garden needs work, serious
attention and a few prunes with the kitchen scissor. Your hair's a little

matte but still very interesting. I just had such a habit of
preoccupation. Triangles unlike the single strands of bent grass. A

bird's wing on either hip bone elegant, one balancing the other but not
droopily. Festoonery. Infatuation. Credible and audible are pretty

grounded but a face can cause a tremor. Morbidity. Tepidity. I am timid now.
Some bird moves and roves in the bower. Do your zipper

up. Let's imagine we're both in love with the same writer. He's a complete
loser. Okay, she's brittle, rather quiet. Why does gender continue

to make such difference? Your thigh quivers. My hair's pretty.
I love this tablecloth even with its berry stains and two wax scabs

patchouli-scented. Lemon geranium and mint over by the echinacea are a floral
segue. I like how gender is almost garden and how gardens cause

wind to tremble. I prefer to think about writing. When my kids are in school
for hours I am a church bell chiming eleven. The guy on the

bus was blind and I held his hand telling him several secrets very
quickly perhaps to make up for preferring space between us.

Disclosure can be alienating. If I look your face over for too long. If I
return to the newspaper and have a paroxysm of self-defeat for the

world is in chaos and what right has the individual to the peculiar
pleasure of hope? Surely you will drop this chapter and get on with your

day. Patience cannot be justified. Credible or audible is fine for an
older story. We're looking for some new hot thing is pointed. It's all

circular with me. I revert to radio. For example, surreptitious crows could
mean something about blackness or an attitude toward religion,

in that you hold just about every element in distrust. Mandible clouds
or marmalade horizon. Certain wings flop over like the insolent grasses

in my garden. Disconsolate. Polar seizures. Can I say anything gentler
about such patio coffee now that it is chilled and old? I knew you were

impatient. I just know how this sort of thing stirs me in the thigh and upward.
The paper and its paroxysms of death are audible and credible

and should be preferred to rumours about writers with secrets. I don't give. I
don't give more than this. Marigolds wilt under too much advice. I'll

pump up the ball, download ballet schedules before the kids get home.
Whatever happens in this next long blink, I am thinking you'd

better scram.

Something Inside Me

I shall probably do that
in the end but now
there is still something inside
me trying to get out
there is time to sit
at home later on www.myspace.com/80192727
I'm a bit better now
I have no fever just
a cough and sniffles but
when I cough it's like
there's something inside me trying
to get out anyway miss
you profile.myspace.com THERE'S SOMETHING INSIDE
ME TRYING TO GET OUT
at 26 years old with
a full arsenal of creative
talent under his belt ShawnQt
has finally swam ashore from
myspace.com/shawnqt Ocean & Monmouth Vamp
meetup Group (Brick, NJ) I'm
Gage 6′1″ I have felt
something inside me trying to
get out since I was
little but until now I
never had the confidence or
anything to let my true
vampires.meetup.com FADE IN I'm scared
too I would never hurt
you It's just there's something
inside me trying to get
out and I don't know

(I REALLY DON'T THINK YOU'RE) STRONG ENOUGH

I

Something inside me was screaming Write
you fool! Tell the whole damned
    world how you
    feel! Something inside
    says there's somewhere
    better than this
Holy one I have something inside me
something nameless I started thinking about
    Yes
Poland and something inside me wanted
to come back Listen to Something
    Inside Me by
    Elmore James for free
    on Rhapsody Something
    inside me wishes
this was photoshopped I closed my
eyes ready to feel something inside
No
me Don't ask me why but
something inside me says Tequila Something
    inside me seeks
    the infinite comfort
    of knowing that
    I am completely
snowbound Something inside me told me
everything would be okay There's something
    Yes
inside me and it's called the
Blues Something inside me has died
    Something inside me
    went There's something
    inside me gnawing
    constantly and I've
yet to put my finger on
it I couldn't articulate it but
No
Star Wars touched something inside me
I can feel something inside me

say I really
don't think I
ate enough Witch's
Brew asks I
feel something inside me stirring Something
inside me some correlation outside me –

2

Cuz when I see you something
inside me burns and then I
        realize I wanna
        come first Something
        inside me gently
        spoke just love
the people the voice said Do
you believe in life after love
        Yes
There is something inside me that
sees waking up anywhere in New
        Jersey as a
        warning sign It
        came inside my
        heart and it
was like something inside me started
to shine Something inside me not
No
rational not pragmatic Something inside me
says I wanna hold you one
        more time but
        something inside me
        keeps saying not
        yet not yet
not yet Something inside me just
told me to Something inside me
        Yes
is exploding to get out and
I don't know what it is
        It's kind of
        like I want
        to do cartwheels

around the neighbourhood
I can feel something inside me
say I really don't think something
No
inside me still made me minor
in Art History There's something inside
    me that pulls
      beneath the surface
      as if something
      inside me lies
empty and broken It was as
if something in those recordings had –

3

Taken hold of something inside me
do you have any more? There's
    something inside me
    you all stare
    but you'll never
    see I smoke
because I just want to feel
something inside me That is how
    Yes
something inside me is filled and
emptied with writing I know I'm
    not stupid and
    I could do
    lots of things
    in my life
but there is always something inside
me that's stopping me from making
No
progress and soon something inside me
leaked between my fingers and spilled
    Something inside me
    knew I'd get
    away with it
    I have an
honest face there's something inside me
that pulls beneath the surface Something

Yes
inside me senses that sex with
a man will leave me feeling
    empty Don't wait
    something inside me
    says go deeper
    I used the
time to finish up *Sputnik Sweetheart*
which really grabbed something inside me
No
There's something inside me I know
there is! And yet something inside
    me slumps tugging
    slowly and relentlessly
    at my attention
    Something inside me
said Oh no This silence with
Osho is too precious Something inside –

4

Me resounded When only its tail's
visible something inside me trembles violently
    For me art
    is something inside
    me The big
    font did look
ugly but something inside me said
Ha you're gonna love this I
    Yes
can feel something inside me say
I really don't think you're strong
    enough no something
    inside me went
    Ping Something inside
    me just went
berserk Something drove me led me
yeah even forced me to sit
No
on those eggs When they're hosted
on a public library system something

inside me kind
of dies Whilst
something inside me
tells me I
couldn't do it all over again
Maybe something inside me would like
    Yes
me to see if I can
do it the right way Bill
    sighs into the
    phone and something
    inside me makes
    my foot tap
Something inside me had slapped me
in the face Honey they put
No
something inside me I don't know
what but maybe because the scared
    look I noticed
    in his eyes
    during spelling dictation
    did something inside
me when I woke the presence
was gone but I felt something –

       .

5

Inside me under the big NEVER
AGAIN sign and something inside me
    just flinched Something
    inside me told
    me how it
    would feel to
fly like a skimmer I think
something inside me just kind of
    Yes
snapped It just changed something inside
me I heard poems totally differently
    I'm a person
    and if there's
    something inside me

and I don't
want it there its right to
life does not trump my right
No
to not have it live inside
me He touches something inside me
    that has never
    felt alive before
    tonight something inside
    me is breaking
but something inside me just hasn't
had enough I wish I did
    Yes
have something inside me something big
and hard rubies would be best
    I've got something
    inside me to
    drive a princess
    blind That night
something inside me stirred Dunno why
I am blogging this but there
No
is something inside me that wants
me to blog this Something inside
    me wanted to
    see how far
    this would go
    I think we
just opened something inside us Something
inside me urged me to draw –

6

A pic based on the final
scene for Sonic the Hedgehog Next
    Gen Something inside
    me was convinced
    that meditation was
    the answer Something
inside me hoped that it wasn't
true Something inside me becomes more

Yes
fluid Something inside me refuses this
glib recitation of unity Something inside
    me still felt
    empty and broken
    As we approached
    the first small
lake I felt something inside me
shift With a stamp of his
No
foot John summoned Shah from the
still water I almost chickened out
    but the something
    inside me was
    still whispering I'm
    a singer and
dancer and I want to show
you I've got something inside me
    Yes
But then as I eat it something
inside me snaps Something inside me
    felt defiled Deeper
    deeper than anyone
    has looked before
    and something inside
me suddenly opened up When I
returned home something inside me made
No
me post an ad on the
Internet Something inside me came I
    really don't think
    you're strong enough
    now For the
    past few days
something inside me has been tugging
at my sleeve saying *Oooh, fall!* –

7

There was something inside me I
want to see a priest You

can feel something
inside me say
Something inside me
begins to stir
barely For some reason something inside
me found this refreshingly different Cuz
Yes
when I see you something inside
me burns Then I realize I
wanna come first
Sometimes I think
I should wash
them but something
inside me says don't wash them
yet not yet I'm watching these
No
people start their own businesses and
it's stirring up something inside me
When I couldn't
take it any
more I begged
for something inside
me while you licked Something inside
me is I guess I could
Yes
say the word revolving It's going
in deep and it's already doing
something inside me
Something inside me
told me that
I had to
come forward and tell my darkest
secrets Something inside me though I
No
didn't want to admit it went
ppffft and disappeared Something inside me
said DRESS UP
YOUR CAT! When
I encountered Mickey
Mantle that weekend
something inside me expanded something inside
me went Ping and I found –

8

Myself typing this I'm running on
some hollow momentum and something inside
        me is punching
        itself out There
        is something inside
        me but what
can it be? Something inside me
goes Bling! Something inside me starts
        Yes
to move I can feel something
inside me say I really don't
        think you're strong
        enough I don't
        remember 'painting' an
        image but just
the act of following with my
eye the motion of my hand
No
which I guess was guided from
something inside me I'm not trying
        to say that
        there's something inside
        me what I
        have inside me
isn't particularly interesting I've watched it
three times and each time something
        Yes
inside me says This is not
right There's something inside me that
        pulls beneath the
        surface there is
        something inside me
        that makes me
want to be a part of
this design community There's something inside
No
me that is a proper little
housewife I love cooking for him
        Something inside me
        burns and then

I realize something
inside me melted
I was about four months of
age when something inside me started–

9

To change Something inside me yells
and then wriggles out with Southern
        force Something inside
        me went Binnnggg!!!
        The PHP key
        unlocked something inside
me that turned me into a
development monkey There's something inside me
        Yes
that clicks into overdrive whenever there's
free stuff involved I think I
        inherited this from
        my older sister –
No
        Yes
No
        Yes
No
        I really don't
        think you're Something
inside me wishes Something inside me
just broke into bits I was
        Yes
informed that I could not run
from something inside me as walls
        started to wiggle
        in their familiar
        yet strange patterns
        Somewhere she says
there is something inside me that
will never desert me again

These poems were written from 2002 to 2007. Several grants from the Ontario Arts Council as well as a Canada Council writer's residency at the University of Windsor in 2004/2005 greatly enabled my writing through this period. Thanks to the English department faculty at the University of Windsor for their collegiality. For two spells, kind Ted Syperek's home on Ward's Island was an appreciable generator of new work. A Canada Council grant in 2008 paved time for final editing.

Thanks to previous publishers of some of these poems. 'Mumsy' is a section from a sequence previously published in *Event*. 'Queen' appeared in *CV2*. The reclaimed texts used in 'The Birdie Went Down' and 'Key Brain Chemicals' were gathered for a festschrift composition for Bill Kennedy and Angela Rawlings at the close of their five-year Lexiconjury Reading series (Toronto). 'Andalou' is reprinted from *Not Egypt* (Coach House, 1989). 'Absurd Picture Show' was posted on *Lemon Hound*. The little latch in 'Turret Door' is a little latch. An earlier version of the text appears in a Roy Miki tribute issue of *West Coast Line*. Letdown and latch are also breastfeeding lingo. A previous version of 'My Attaché Case' appeared in *Lichen*. 'The Hoity-Toity Supplements' is a timely tribute to the beauty of fertility and the Enough! decision. Hours of spontaneous counting arrived as a body operative during my first labour. Sections were previously published in the *Capilano Review* and *grimm*, and the whole suite is online (text and audio) at www.testreading.org, with thanks to Mark Truscott. 'Something Inside Me' was previously published as a chapbook by In Case of Emergency Press (2007). Thanks to Tim Conley and Clelia Scala.

The large pink bowtie in 'Used' is part of Silas's homemade Mr. Pringles costume. Also, my mom was a Big Sinatra Fan and used to take me to Eaton's, when department stores were real. Hind milk is the richer milk you want the baby to get to, maybe for the fats of memory in it. 'Hope you' read Kathy Acker and other writers while they are alive and licking. 'Lovely One' is for anyone who aspires to live near a river. Acknowledgement to Martin Morris. 'Apartments That Reek' is for a fellow named Victor whose parents would want him to have the first floor. 'What stirs?' refers to poetry's backyard for fourteen years at 245 1/2 Markham, RIP beloved Capp and Jal buried there. 'Strong Enough' reminds me of a phrase from the song by Cher. Everything on the Internet is already 'Something Inside Me.'

Many thanks for employment and camaraderie to Lee Gowan at the University of Toronto School of Continuing Studies Creative Writing Program and to Trevor Owen at Writers in Electronic Residence (WIER). Thanks to Maureen Hynes, and to Barry Olshen and Ann Hutchison at Glendon College. Thanks to the growing community of guest poets and registrants who have passionately participated in 'Influency: A Toronto Poetry Salon.' Special thanks and affection to Rachel Zolf. Thanks as well to my Creative Writing students over the last three years – I continue to learn a great deal.

Thanks to Margaret McDonnell for the oak tree view from May 2007–. Gratitude to the Christakos family for financial and moral support 1962–. Thank you to the extended Gee family 1987–. And also: for encouragement through the strangely dark days of 05–06, thanks to many cherished friends. To Freda Martin, much appreciation.

My sincere gratitude to Kevin Connolly for a scrupulous and nourishing editing process, and to Alana Wilcox for tremendous dedication and consistently wise advice. Many thanks as well to Christina Palassio, Evan Munday, Stan Bevington and everyone at Coach House Books.

Thank you to Bryan Gee for cover design collaboration. The front cover image is an anatomical lithograph (colour plate illustration) by Antoine Chazal from the multi-tome *Anatomie Pathologique* by Jean Cruveilhier (1829–35). The back cover image is borrowed from a 1958 *Life* magazine article on the spanking new and efficient 'Living-Kitchen.' The inside front cover image is from a March 1948 article in *Mechanix Illustrated* on 'Pills That Increase Your Intelligence' (I'd like a few) accessed via Google, searching 'a glass of milk.' The image on the inside back cover is from an illustrated annual called the *Wonder Book of Wonders*.

Ongoingly, and with love, I am grateful to Bryan Gee and our children, Clea, Silas and Zephyr, for contemplating artistic temperament. I am forever in your attaché cases.

Margaret Christakos is attached to this earth. She has published six previous collections of poetry, including *Sooner* (2005, shortlisted for the Pat Lowther Award) and *Excessive Love Prostheses* (2002, winner of the ReLit Award for Poetry), as well as the recent chapbooks *Adult Video* (Nomados, 2006) and *My Girlish Feast* (Belladonna, 2006). She is the author of the Trillium-shortlisted novel *Charisma*. Raised in Sudbury, Ontario, she has lived in Toronto since 1987.

Typeset in Lexicon 2
Printed and bound at the Coach House on bpNichol Lane, 2008

Edited by Kevin Connolly
Interior design by Bryan Gee and Alana Wilcox
Cover by Bryan Gee
See page 102 for information on cover images

Coach House Books
401 Huron Street on bpNichol Lane
Toronto, Ontario M5S 2G5

800 367 6360
416 979 2217

mail@chbooks.com
www.chbooks.com